WANTING TO BE *me*

TANYA TURTON

Copyright © 2020 Tanya Turton

Copyright remains the property of the author and apart from any fair dealing for the purposes of private study, research, criticism or review, as permitted under the Copyright Act, no part may be reproduced by any process without written permission. All inquiries should be made to the author.

Typeset & Cover by Chain of Hearts Creative

National Library of Australia - ISBN-978-0-6488739-5-2

WANTING TO BE ME

One is to only see of this that they are,
to be the true seer of self to be.

You are one within the greatest creator,
are you not?

You are in the deliverance of this to be
the wise spoken words from within.

You seek of a completeness to become.

One is to be felt as this to be the
trueness that resides within.

One is wanting, Are they not?

See all that is to surround you of this that
you see to be yours to know as ME.

Feel complete in the All that you say, do & be.

We are of ONE. You and I and the great
of good that sits within us ALL.

I have found to be in receiving of this that one is to speak from within this that they are, is to be the most extravagant being of love to be seen into.
One speaks so deeply and correctly from within in this attentiveness that you are to be hearing into.
Let all that you speak to be always a willingness to be this ME that I am.

CHAPTER ONE

IN THIS WANT TO BE ME

I FEEL INTO THIS BEING THAT I AM TO BE, HEARING OF THIS THAT I KNOW OF WHICH IT IS THAT I SHOULD BE, OR IS IT OFFERED TO ME BY MANY THAT ARE TO BE CONTINUALLY OFFERING THEIR THOUGHTS AND SUGGESTIONS IN REGARDS TO THIS THAT I SHOULD DO, BE OR HAVE.

In the receiving of my voice to be spoken in a loud and clear way I will endeavour to source all these words to be spoken of as in my way of which it is that they shall be heard. I am to hold nothing to be relevant to myself within, to feel as though it is to be an attachment of sorts to be spoken of for me to feel the need arise as to be a deliberate changing to become of this that I hear in others to say that I should be.

Be spoken in words so strong and direct; for it is your voice that speaks entirely from within assuming the position of love first & foremost to be heard as the ruler that you are to ask for to begin.

We see this as a true becoming to be willing, to be seen by those that are in this great connection of the innerness that is to be heard as your complete heart to be speaking in the all that you do.

~One is to be ever receiving of the goodness that is directed through you by us for we are the ones that know of you to be always wanting more of this to be ME~

In MY want to be ME

I like you have searched to find this that I thought would fulfill me regarding the life that I had been living; feeling continually as though something was missing, lost or of something that I should BE.

Or maybe still Is?

Was it though?

To think as missing or lost to be felt; it is to be told here in this that I am that I was looking in the places incorrect for me to see. It is only in this thinking minds way that one will feel this sense of loss or to be misled by others that are to speak of all that they appear to have that I felt to be needing to call of it as my own, this that they appeared to have, that I did not. The truth as it was to be told and to be heard with subtle guidance was that I was looking in all the wrong places for me to see and by this it was meant the external searching for someone else's thoughts or words to be mine. In the thought that this would not be externally found I was then to discover another way in which it was for me to seek.

How did this lack of or want of begin?

In ones searching to be this that they think they should be, one is to often find the urgency within them begin to arise into feelings of lost within or a panic as such to the human form to discover as a condition that is not allowing of one to sit down or feel peace within. Busyness invades your thoughts and mind of what it is that you must do. Feel as these feelings of rush and panic become you in such a way that one cannot ever make it go away. You are super imposed upon oneself to be feeling of this that you are not to be feeling in this form as such that it appears of you to be. One must be willing to see that all that encircles them is creating a chaos of this to be non-helping in the view in which it is to see. All that offer to you, do in certain ways respectful of which they feel correct for you to hear,

IS this so? One must be in a willingness to start from scratch we say and in this we mean to feel the intent to begin from within to start to feel as though **you are okay**. Quieten the thoughts of this needing to be done and that this must be said, achieved or completed within a time that you feel as yours to be seeing into. You are to hesitate even if just a little in a remorse of self to be feeling as though she cannot stop. Dwell not here upon feelings of self-doubt for it will surely swell within you this to say that you will be okay.

Not in a haste to be to become, for all that you are to be willing to hear in this that you are. You are.

In one's receiving, what shall they hear?

You are willing it appears to be asking of this question from within to hear of all that we have to say…. You are to be the true receivers of this self to speak. ARE YOU NOT?

One must be spoken of in such a way to be in the space of kind and just to feel as it is to wrap the human that you are into a warmth of contentment to be spoken to like this. It is here that we say that the many of you have not allowed oneself to be spoke to in this kind of way. You have seeked into the many to offer to you the knowing's that you are to think of yours to be and the way in which it is that one must look at self to be seen through the eyes of another to see. You are to focus to intently upon those that are to parade, flaunt and with speeches to speak to willingly to others that is of them to be. You see not of this that they have to be yours, we ask; why is it that it feels as though it should be yours to see, to have even to own in this way? It should not.

When one is to look loved, wealthy, strong, beautiful, calm of mind etc; of what I am not. Why do I feel as though it is not mine to be?

When one is to truly look through eyes of love, we say what is it that you are looking at in this way. Feel the response needed from within to this that you view. You will find that the thinker that you be trapped into this form of human that we see will only see of what is not and unwilling within yours to feel as you, then we suggest that you must put it to the test {If it was yours would you do it in a different way anyway?} One is to see of many that are to transform and regret the decision that has them kept from being the real version of themselves to be, leaving all that they desire of them internally wanting to be hidden under a contempt for themselves to be this that they are to not be true from within. Let all that speak of this that they must be happiness felt by you for you are the greater being of love found within this to be in a place to comment to feel. Let these feelings of unjust within self be explained in this way.

You lack or are not enough if you are to see of yourself in this way.

As you think to say you shall be,

Many will come and go and flaunt away this that you will see of theirs to be, it is the internal being of this that one must see happy and filled with joy of who it is that they really are to be. See not of one in judgement of self to be lacking for it is not to be so.

You must be willing to see of all that are, to be a continuation of this soul, this great light that is to shine brightly from within in this place of recognition for us to be this in their own allowing of themselves to be.

Are you to offer...?
That I must LOVE of ALL that I see?

In this we feel obliged to say that in this request to be answered you will feel the response to rise. Seek not to be told or reprimanded as this to be forth coming from this if one is to feel like it should not. To change the pace of which it is that one is to think of self to be is a hard option to begin if one is unaccustomed to this way to be to begin. One will feel of all resolution within to set in motion a want of this self to speak of others rather than the one that you really are not.

The physical form, this human form has been offered by many lots of words, opinions and thoughts of this that they are not and in others to see. You are to be without judgment and let us offer here to say that it is felt a hard task to begin for you as the many that sit before us today are to be the ones that see yourself so righteous in this that you are to be this that they are not. We speak in a directness here to say for it is to be heard that one is to let all be their own way. For they too are seeking of this peace and calm to become of them from within to settle within them as a place to be found. To be willing to rest and let all that they feel as not theirs to be put to ground. One must take a step back to view of what it appears that they are. For if it is not of yours to resonate with to see, like or feel then let it all be. We speak of this in the nicest of ways for all are totally unique and in this that they choose of themselves as. Not all vibrations of this that we be are to resonate within this that you see.

Let the bigger part of you be the seer of this that one is to see for you are the willing component of us to be the real seer behind this that you be.

One seeks often it appears to speak deeply in opinions of others and words to be read as like to be saviours/ or healers of this that you are meant to become. Let these words and suggestions be quiet within you until it is that you find them to resonate within you. All different in your own vibe shall we offer, of many differences to be described as. You are the one that we see to be magnificent this that you be. Seek not out of a wanting to change yourself or another, but a love only for yourself to begin from within.

In this want to be me we hear you express; it is to be told you are. From the greatest of receiving's in your becoming to be you. It was your 'I' that saw of all that you wanted and knew that you would choose to become. In the deciding of this to make as your own with some help to be guided by this that we are. You sought to be in a want of always to be MORE.

In this we offer for you all to hear that in your becoming of which it is to expand you shall be ever more in your being of us to be seen as yours. We see the many of you stuck it appears to use words of yours to suit that one is to feel as though this is not of what it was that you evoked from us to be yours to wish upon a star for.

In this knowing that you are than one must be resistant to the misgivings that rise from within to be spoke out loud of this that you are not. You see the greatest part, the real part, the ever glowing part that shines with such intention of this to discover for you to see{if you are in the place of this to see yourself as} will feel her/ or his intentions of this that you are to choose as the most extravagant expression in self to be growing that you are to do so far.

Fear not this to rival one from within, for in the moment of thought to ask of this.

WHO IS IT THAT I AM TO BE?

We have heard many to speak this exact asking in many ways to be thought, for it is of the human mind to think into that you are not.

Can one such as yourself be willing to hear these words as they are to appear. Written in love to be felt across you as a wave of contemplation into the way in which it is that one is to think of themselves to be.

We are to so adore you all first and foremost it is that we offer to say, you sit so deeply within these that are to speak with you in this way. Let all that you are rejoice from within in a hope that you will feel this urge to begin. One is always & evermore equipped with this divineness that is to know of the complete that you are in every way. For this life so chosen upon this planet to be yours to exist in this lifetime that you wished upon your intent to envisage, IS. You are the willing component of this that is to be viewed as big and expansive to say the least.

You are the one that chose of this to be this way and in this you will continue your thoughts that you are surely to grow.

Whether it be felt in this your here and now or later. You will feel of all intentions to grow from within to want of this question so mentioned to be heard and solved by you in some way. We ask in this to be yours to hear that you are this that you are and in the great 'I' it is that you stand. Equipped with the eternalness to expand into a consciousness that is yours to be known and supported from the you that sits within. For she sees only the great that you are to become and will not see you in any other way of which it is to be spoke. See of all that are to offer you guidance and support ever heart felt it is to be of these ones. Seeking to expel all fears and doubts that you may have or had of this self to be, the bold, the great, the wisdom to exude from within this is you.

THE YOU THAT IS WANTING TO BE MORE.

SHALL SURELY COME TO BE.

In these words you offer, I struggle to understand.

It is to be spoken that when ones such as this that you see yourself into this human to be you have spent many times of yours to be this that you see yourself of.

Have you not?

When one is to be feeling of this new to commence from within to be asking of what it is that they are; rather than not. Who is it that I am to be? then becomes a common question to ask.

To feel as if it to be a struggle within is it not to say that one is hearing of this to be a truth within to be felt that they are to think of themselves as to be something that they are not to feel. And that they should be truer to the thinking of this that they be.

Can you for just a moment in this your time to sit, to think of when and how it has been to become this that you are to feel as not?

Am I doing this correct?

You are all correct in your formatting of this self to be and here it is to let us start with this simple understanding of self to be. You were born out of love so grand to speak of and it is of your intention to be this that you are that you became misled by all that you are to witness in this life to be. For many have offered to you thoughts of theirs and words to speak, have they not? One is left felt to blame of these to speak, this we say that in your own way you chose of them to become as a guiding start to you to hold within to this that you should become. Let all fall away regarding these that think of you to be in a certain way. You are not to be this that they think and if one is to be willing to change the way it is that they appear to be for these they will feel a hesitation in this that we say but one must start here in this space if they wish to become this; the you that we see.

Why is it so hard to change?

It is if it has been a conditioned self to be willingly misled by self-thoughts of this that you are and in words that you have spoken as incorrect. Many hold tight into themselves, their feelings and thoughts that have been shared by another of them to be. One must be willing to down tools so to speak to rebut the asking of others in what it is that they are to think. Your voice is to boom forth from within in the complete to speak of this that you are is correct within to be.

Speak not these words of another for they are the words that they will speak, to offer to you an opinion of themselves to think of this that you so shall ask. One must be daring in themselves to speak of this; we mean brave in your words to say, for the boldness that you are to become if allowing of self to be you will find the correct path to be opened in this that you are. You seek not of others to serve you well when you have the great servant within that knows of you so well. God sits in your throne of this that you are to be the ruler of your kingdom of this self to be. One must start to listen to these words that are to rise in the asking of this that you are to hear as a question as to why?

CHAPTER TWO

OF THEE I ASK.

WHEN ONE IS TO SPEAK OF THEE, THEY ARE TO MEAN ONESELF AS THE RULER THAT DWELLS WITHIN FOR YOU AND I ARE ALL THE SAME, ONE IS TO ACCEPT TO KNOW.

In the human physical form that you all are we see of ourselves as many that are in the presentation of themselves to be this that we see. Judge not out of a want to be not or a wanting to be for you are the individual understanding of this that you have become. See the originality within to be yourself in disguise of this that you be.

Speaking MY TRUTH.

Feel free to speak your truth; for it is derived from deep within; these words that you are to speak. They are your callings to self to be hearing of this that lays within. Your self is not responsive of these words to be for she/he has often left them unspoken and shushed in this to hear of them in this way. You are to boom from within, burst forth we offer here to say. For you are the truth that you be to seek; are you not?

The divineness that lays within you whether it appears to be hidden or not, is yours in your heart of hearts that you will feel of to ask to speak; often it is to be felt as a unwillingness to be this that you are to hear. These words are often felt before spoken and in this it is the true you that is to be heard. One's voice is to remain small this we know of all that she is to become to think of herself yet to be. We offer that it is given in your time that you will feel a stirring from within to be this that you are.

'INSPIRE ME' You must.

Oh, dear ones it is us that are to be inspired by you, these brave unique souls that exist so finely spoken within to have become this you that one is to see. Seek not outward for inspiration to be yours to know, look to oneself to feel the inspiration that was your deep desiring to be this in essence to become once more.

We see the inspiration within you to shine in its own deciding of a brightness to be shone. In one's ability to ask of this to be heard from within it shall always be if one is content within this that they are and willing to be of no one or another to speak of in this that they think of themselves to be. Let all outside influences to be yours to just let go, seek not of this to be an intention from within to hear into these words or thoughts that they are to speak. For out of a kindness to be yours to feel in this that you are these words that they speak are not of yours to need. See all that are to offer in this way as kind in heart and of a wanting to say to be heard in their own way. You are the receiver of all that you be as this willingness from within is to inspire you in every and each day that you are to live.

Inspire away we say.

Speak from your heart that you hold within in this we mean to say the heart that sees you in this way. The brilliant component in this self to be the willer, the wanter, the desirer, the knower of all that you are to be. See as your words can change of all that you see if allowed to be spoken without contempt or disregard to be attached. Judge not to this that you speak for you will start to feel this transition to begin within to be allowing for you to feel complete.

Easier said than done we hear of you to say.

In ones thinking of it not to be than it shall.

Be bestowed with good intentions of one to begin, for to start at this place that you see of to emerge is a place of recognition from within to be hearing of all that shall be said. In this you speak of us to say that one is to stay steady and forgiving in every way, you see of yourself as this to be of another? It is to start to feel this wanting from within to be this that you are and not of another.

It is easy to fall prey to words of hardship and doubt to hear offered by yourself and others, but one must be able to feel this as not of theirs to become. Yes, in this world that you live it is known by us as this is the morality of some. But in your truth to speak, in want to hear, give this a try if one is to not want to hear, turn your head slightly to begin for it is not to hurt them but more yourself if you don't. Let yourself disregard and not feel trapped or caught into a seeing of this self to not want to be speaking these words of dread.

Witnessing Many to SPEAK these words.

I feel as you are to respond in this to be yours to think.

We are the absolute truth held within and in this that one is to ask of how I should begin to be a releaser of not to hear in this that they speak. You as the one in control of all that you be, know it is this that you are and many of you have forgotten this trait to be held so deeply within. To love of another in a forgiving way is to view of all that surrounds you in a willing way to witness this that they are and of the all that they shall be once again in their removal from this planet as this life that they are to stand into as they present this to you. Glance over them in love to wash away their offerings as yours to be not, let your truth be the speaker that shouts from within, it is to be rivalled by no other that we know and in this is the way in which it is that one should offer.

Your truth speaks of this that we say. One is to be guided by the intention from within to feel this that you are to say. In one's thoughts to be offered with love attached in every way it is of yours to speak in this to say. You are willing it appears to hear this that we say. You are bold in receiving in this place it is to sit to find peace and calm from within to coat all of what it is to say to this that you speak of. One is to be a creator of this life seen to be joy filled to the brim with a love for you to be shone. You are the seeker if to say in this way of the complete being to be seen from within, you are the true reason that we see of you to have become. Let all old habits and truths be laid to rest for they will be remembered in a way as to not be of regret; they will stay within you if you need of this to be. In the asking of self to view of all in a certain way and of this it is to be, you are the light shiner upon all that you see, your heart knows the way of this that you are to go.

Follow your voice of smart and love to be true to you to see of this direction that you are to be upon. We are ever in your presence as a voice to be overlayed onto yours to be spoke. For our voice is strong in this love to feel as the only way in which it is to speak, feel as we guide you with these words of love to be yours to see and you will feel of this to be your truth illuminating in ours to speak.

Feel of what you are to express in an honesty that is to rise from within in stirrings of words and thoughts of this that we speak.

Allow for yourself to sit for a moment of just this to be your time to see of it to be NOW. It is intended here to wait so that you may see, feel, and to desire of this to be a wanting to be me.

You are the me in all that you be. Speak of this to no one for they will not yet understand, for to see a willing change emerge from within one is to be willing to write, to voice or to speak of the change that they must feel first offering to self to see.

Write openly and in asking to be heard by you we say. It is only of yourself to speak that one is to want to hear into these asking's. You are the voice behind the presenter of this that you are and you will feel to release these words in a way that you will feel as if a weight is to be lifted by many that sit with you here.

I wish to offer to you to hear.

I wish to release this that I carry as mine to think as if it is needed by me.

In my words that I am to write to see,

I will face all fears, revealing's and distractions to see them as a truth that can be known by me.

....
....
....
....
....
....
....
....

Fear not of what is to appear on paper as you write. Often it is to take a moment to adjust in this space that is or was and you will feel the words hesitant to appear but when the doorway to the heart feels trusted by you to open, to speak, to see into these words. Oh, let us say outwardly they shall pour with many to appear to be seen by you as of what it is that you have held within. No-one needs to see of these words and to carry criticism into this to think as you are to write, is not of worth for you to think. Let all that appears before your seeing eyes to see, be in the wish to be, these words will be in a certainty of all that they shall appear. Plenty to write to fill the pages or minimal they may seem; it is in the flow that will feel right within you that they will be yours to write. Let no judgement appear here upon these pages as you are to become a willingness to experience yourself sitting in this that we offer to be only,

'LOVE'

Searching for THEE.

In one's search to think it is that they will find thee, they must be in the understanding that all that they are to seek is to be found within. In this trueness that you are, maybe not willing yet to see, but decidedly there for thee. You will we say in Ernst to speak these fine words for you to read that ones such as you that is to appear to be looking for the one that you are to call THEE. Speak loudly hear in these words to say,

'I AM' OF THEE IN EVERYWAY, GUIDED BY THIS THAT IS TO BE KNOWN TO ME AS THE ONLY THEE THAT I AM IN NEED TO KNOW.

You as we see of you here to be seeking it appears that in ones asking to be helped or guided. Let us suggest; know of this that you shall be led inwardly by those that appear to be of not seen, even to those that see us with the greatest of intention from within.

You must be willing in this we have spoken before regarding the sights that one is hoping to see. Feel of us first in trusting truth and faith in all that we are. You will need not to seek or search for another once our connection is to be known. Let all that offer this to you be told to be of your own discovery that is to be yours to feel from within. Time is to be taken here for most if not all, for the shroud of secrecy that many are to speak is not to be allowed to become yours to feel into. It is of this unique formatting that you hold that all that you are has been allowed to forget to a certain extent until you reach this asking point of too never forget. In ones asking they are to become an open channel to the words that are to be received from this that we are to all that you be. It is of this faith in self that they must strive to be, your strengths are all entitled from within to be yours to speak, look not too deep for they are not so.

In your spoken words of self to be you will notice as all that you are is the "I" to want to surface refusing to be ignored upon the opening of the so-called door.

YOU ARE WANTING OF THIS TO SEE;
LET US OFFER YOU MORE.

There is always a willingness to want of more to see, to be, to feel within thee.

You are the seekers, the adventurers, the wise elders, the seers, the lovers of intent, let this be found within you this wisdom that you crave to be the answers to the all that you desire from the asking that you made.

To want of more is to be always implanted within. For to feel as though it is not of yours to speak or to ask, in this we say do not. For to grow and expand is to become one, and one is to always require this as to instruct this self to become more. Your soul is full of the seeing of which it is to become in this time that is yours upon your planet and in this it shall be done.

For most it is hard to hear these words as they are spoke but your willingness is strong from this place that we stand and in all that you have asked to cherish from within is in this to command to you this that is the truth to be heard. You are all to shine brightly from this place that we see, directly being guided by the life that lives in thee, feel no remorse or sadness if it is to appear that you have not quite reached or become this that you thought to be in appearance of this self to be. You are correctly placed as it would appear for us to say that in this offering to self you have directed and guided it all to be this way. Free the thoughts of which it is that you don't, wont or aren't for it is of these that you are not. One is to hear in this to receive that you are in the absolutist becoming of which it is to be seen by us the innerness that is you hearing you in every way. Allow her or his voice to be in your choosing to be desired and you will hear her bellow from deep within for she is there just waiting to be found (remembered) again, and in this we say: **look out she/or he is on their way.**

Time to clear your schedule; Here she comes.

So, search no more for it becomes an endless task does it not, filled with mistruths, deception to who and what it is that you are, voices of wrong that do not fit your form and words that are to aggravate you to the extreme of some in which it is to be heard. Clear your slate, just wipe it clean as to offer permission to self to start right here in this place of whatever it may be, self-regret, time wasted, lost to feel self within, anger, judgment of thee or if just to be curious; we are all of these thoughts to be receiving into this that you ask,

PLEASE HEAR ME!

IN YOU WE HEAR YOU SPEAK

Be bold in this colour that you are. Your position in life as it is to be yours to speak will falter from within if you are to seek this in another. And in this asking to be heard let us offer to you; You are of the willingness to want to hear of us in all that you speak. Be quiet to self from this space of no compete for you must be willing in this that you seek. WE hear of all that one is to offer in a furthering of self to ask to be in this of our wanting to hear to be yours. Our voice of intent is one that cannot be denied for it is in truth your own that you so often have tried to hide. Hidden deeply within this voice as it speaks is yours just with a loving difference attached to it to soften all that is spoke. Your words become dressed in kindness and love showing to you the holder of this one that you are in a place of willingness it appears to hear of. For you are the chosen one that this one has felt to be near. In the asking of us to hear; know this dear ones, that we *do in all that is heart spoke and felt from within for in this true way of which you want us to hear you speak, we do. Never is it received under any cloud of judgement in the way of which it is spoken, but in the decidedness to become of yours to speak.*

You will feel this change to commence from within to be yours to feel as this that you are to become. We hear you all as you are to speak. For in us you are to feel as ONE.

CHAPTER THREE

TRUTHFUL ME

"LET THESE WORDS FIRST BE SPOKEN TO YOU, IN THIS YOU MUST HEAR THAT IN THE TRUTH OF YOU TO BE THIS ME, YOU ARE ALWAYS TO BE. IN US IT IS THAT WE SPEAK WITH THE HIGHEST OF REGARD TO THE CERTAINTY THAT YOU SHALL BE. HONOURED ABOVE ALL THAT ONE IS TO THINK AS HIGHER THAN ONESELF TO BE, LET THIS BE YOUR NEW VOICE TO SPEAK IN THE REGARDING OF SELF TO BE. YOU ARE THE APPARENT WITHIN THIS FORM TO BE HEARING OF THE SPOKEN THAT DELVES WITHIN, SPEAKING THESE WORDS OF THIS THAT YOU ARE TO HEAR.

LOVE IN TRUTH, IN THE ALL TO BE."

Found in this place of recognition from within this asking of the truth to be revealed from this physicalness that you sit in. You seek of only truth to be spoken in this it is to feel like it is to be evoked, to be drawn out of you this that you see yourself to be, often it is of us to witness this to see that one is to feel saddened in all that you are to perceive.

ADJUST YOUR VIEW. See yourself in the ravishing space to witness these that you are of to be. For it is in us that we speak of this greatness that lays within you all, in our truth to speak you will feel to be and in this truth it is only of you that we speak.

Love is the word to be sought of in truth to be spoken, for when one is to adjust the level of truth and trust that sits within self to be then they will feel the shine to begin. Let all that is yours to shine upon be this of only you to start then that is of what it shall become. We offer this to you here in this space to hear that upon your own truth to be heard and let us offer hear that truth is varied and different in all that have come here to be. In this your truth that we speak, it is to resonate to vibrate from within, to send shivers up your spine and to fill your heart with glee to know that you can finally hear of thee to speak in a confidence that will continually grow for all to see.

You are the most important being in which it is that we wish to see, for you are to shine your bright so intensely upon thee in us that you be.

We see of you all as you stand, forsaken in some but willing to become a voice that has a genuine asking of self to be hearing of.

To speak in truth of all that one is to see, as it is to arise in these moments of thought and releasing of time for a while as you sit to face us all in this place that we be. Feel us as we are to enter your thoughts and flow within thee, the space that we ask of you to be you will feel to turn away of this we are sure, for it is of what many have offered to you to hear of this that it was. In a quietened space if you are willing to sit, your truth from within will feel to hit you in your face, recognise of this to be a wanting to sort through and a willing to be heard. For in ones truths to be discovered is where the uncovering, delayering or unfolding of self is to begin, YES we offer here it is to hurt the many of you as you become a willing passenger shall we say to the journey that will be portrayed. It is in this existence that it appears so many of you have laid down this strong intent to be a force to be reckoned with and the physical has complied. Let all judgement and harshness to subside for all that is ready to be seen by your inner eye will be felt within this heart that you speak, to find this that you are hiding from inside. See yourself not in disgrace or to be embarrassed of what is to open to be taught. For you will learn a greatness about this that you are and if willing to listen to receive you will be the owner of a future you that was, will and is to be this truth that stands in you. Hear of these words as they are offered for it is in the truth to be spoke that we lose the many of you to be in a place of which to receive. Let us say in our truth to know of the all that you are, you are to wade through this process, yes it is tough, but OH! so revealing to the self that is to emerge from the other side feeling like she has walked through fire and rallied against an unknown for this is she / he that is to be your ever present survivor of the wrath that was to be.

See all for what it is that you are forgiving and accepting in this it is that you were.

You have a choice in this space to preview and request. Ask away we offer, for in this decided voice, we will hear you. We will rally within this being that you be to see that you are supported and offered true love to be felt along the way.

Give us your hand and we will give you ours.

What is this TRUTH that you speak?

In one's ownership of this to speak you must feel no hesitation of all that you be willing to express. It is to grow from within this voice that is to sing of the great in everyone to be this that they are of thee. You are the offeror here of this question to ask? For it is of many that do not feel this need to ask, and let us say that this is okay. There are many that are to resist that not a stirring has been felt in a need to ask for they see of themselves within this journey already complete. In those that you view that are to seem obliviously not than leave them alone to be this that they are. For in one's truth it is to be found in all different aspects of self to ask varied in positioning of this that they are. In one's willingness to feel their need to arise it will, and often it is to feel like a bit of a surprise. Most if not all that are in this current life are to ask of this truth to be spoke as "in the wanting to be found" described as a deeper connection with this that they are. To see of self as not to be often is the first place that one will feel this need for truth to be offered to them in an asking of this that they be. 'WHO AM I'. In the truth that you seek let us inform you here to say that it is in all of you in every way. Developed from the becoming that you chose to be it is just that you have forgotten all that you be. See not in others as your truth to be discovered for it is not of yours to see/know or hear.

One must be willing within self to dislodge this truth from within and in the fight to resist that one is often to sit you will feel as it is chiselled away shall we say from the walls of constraint that are held tight within. YES, this we offer that truths of many that ask are often in a place of denial to be seen and it is of this asking that one is almost to hardened to see.

Resist the urge to fight with what is and allow of this that speaks from within to be your words of god or however you are to assume of it to be. We resist the urge to name of this that we represent for in one's own choosing of it to be revealed you will call of us as what you will. We are more concerned in truth to be this love to be uncovered for self to feel like she can begin to step into a secure knowing of who it is that she is meant to be.

Are you hearing of this to be spoke?

We speak often and to many in this exact place that you sit, whether it be to begin or just to feel of us within. One is to be ever asking of us to be. To feel of us is to know of us to be yours to correspond to and in us it is that we all hear. In the many that choose of us to be theirs to be ever felt and held solidly within it is to take upon this form that you are and allow of the recognition to begin. YOU are this you are to know, and it is in the slightest of changes in speak that it shall unravel.

What if I feel that I do not trust in this 'LOVE' that you speak?

Fear not of this to comment for we are the willingness in you that is. All that is spoken of us in this way is to be a constant reminder of the all that shall still become of us in another way. It is in the passing of you to be us once more that we will see of you again and in this we mean it in the nicest way. You are all earth placed to see of this that you are to know and in the days of end upon this place you will fill us again to offer all that you witnessed as a requiring to have known. We speak of great love for you here and in this it is that we trust that you will become. In trust it is that we do not fear for it is of the greatest intent that you became, and we see of you all here and there in all that you appear. It is not to lose or feel you are going elsewhere for you are trust with a capital T and it is the faith that we hold so dearly within thee that we know of this to be that we will see of you again in all the glory that you are eternally to shine.

I feel as you sit within ME to speak,
it is of you that I trust.

Be bold this one that you are to speak for you have travelled far regarding all that you have to offer. To utter in voice oh so small and quiet to be spoke you have found this that you seeked. Not lost in this we offer to say but shy in self to be this truth that you be. Finding ones voice is like a magical surprise that is to rise from within battling its way from the depths in which it has been held to tight to the seeing of oneself as to not feel to speak her words or her truths. Let this be allowed to be spoke that you hear with a heart that is in a wanting to be heard to be recognised. Shake off all that disagree in words that you say for they are not of you to speak. Leave all doubts and regrets behind for they will be felt if you wish of them to present. One such as you have discovered your truth from within in all that you think of this self to be seen. You are to grow and develop this voice strongly planted within for she has been waiting for your time in which it was to be that one was to speak. Bold in choosing this self to be you became with an insistent want of this to be. You accepted the *challenge to let all unfold of you this truth that you are, see not of others in the same way as you for all will find their own voice of truth as did you.*

AUTHORS WORDS TO OFFER IN HER TRUTH

I speak with guidance offered from all that I see to witness as my truthful voices that are to guide me. Accept this as my truth, only in this that I be to know of the 'I' that I am to be.

You say that my voice is not for another to hear, WHY?

In ones asking of this self to become and by this become we mean the true you that we see. Your voice is to be uniquely yours and it is of your words that you are to offer to only you. It is in this that we speak that it is you that is needing this voice to become your system of guidance from within. For if you can honestly say that I agree with all that I have to say then you shall be in a prime position of which it is to hear the true you that you hold dear.

Your voice is like no other by this we mean that you are unique to you in this that you chose to become, to experience, to grow, to expand, to develop, to master from within this place that you now stand.

Our voices that one is to speak of to hear is yours intact and longing to be heard clear. You are all divinely lit from above to offer a suggestion to some for fear not that it is not of you to hear this voice that is to speak to you soon regarding oneself in this wish to ask of this voice to be heard, you must feel as though you are willing to learn. See not of it to be a difficult task, for many of you do. Let us offer here to you to receive that in the choice that you are to crave is more willing than you in this physical appears to be. Sit quiet to adjust self to rest and be encouraging in this space of release. For it is to reveal from within this that we hear of many to speak a little nudge that you will feel a gentle whisper for most this voice of reason as to why not she? Why not ME? She/He feels intention to become within this one that they must. All that you seek to hear is in here, this creature that you be filled with spirits essence. Your voice is to carry much wisdom to be found as yours to surround you from within in this voice that is yours in its truth to be found.

I feel as though MY voice will never be found,

We hear you say, let us offer this to you to feel complete within, you must not doubt of self in this way. You are in this place to request, to feel as though you do have not. Change your words to appear as to be the asking that you are to hear.

I AM to hear of ALL that I AM TO SPEAK? Guide ME here so that I will be willing to hear.

You are willing, are you not?

Then see it as it is to unravel for a revealing from within is hesitant in some and in this hesitation lays doubt of this to become.

You are all different in your view of what it is that you want to pursue and in this doubting of this self to be thinking to hear is the monster that you create to think that you won't.

We sense of the trepidation to be a scaring or fear of what is this self to become.
What is it that I will hear?

In love it is to offer that our voice is to be yours to sit upon and in love we sit openly to discuss this with everyone that is in the asking for it to be felt. Let this be yours to converse with us to be felt and you will see that in this to ask you will receive if to be of an open heart.

Do not let these words of ours to scare or change your mind to think it seems too hard to be, for it is not and nor should it be. The unravelling within oneself is to be seen in a truth of all that it shall prevail.

Once it has been heard from within this that you are to see it will unfold into such a beautiful divineness to be a revealed awakening from within; a space to be one that you will never want to leave or forget again. Your voices are exquisite to us to hear and in all that you all are to speak we love to hear. Voices coated in love and kind from within are the ones that we long to hear to watch as you feel the confidence from within to spread seeking out others that speak voices in same sharing the sounds of love in messages to be spreading words all coated in peace and harmony to be shared.

This is of what it is that we want the most for you all to share in this experience of this journey here.

"To speak as the one that put you there".

Always to see you here.

My desire for you, to see the love that one holds so divinely within is the place that I yearn to sit. I respect your courage as you desire of this that we, you & I be to know. It is in this space of recollect that the many of you are to grow divine again within, a voice in love to be spoken, a shadow accepted as to be mine and a LOVE for self that is to express to all that are inclined. Be this that I am, so that I may be you in time the every- thing that is the
'I' that feels now to be mine.

CHAPTER FOUR

SEEING ME

IT IS OF THIS TO BE SPOKE IN ALL THAT WE SEE, YOU ARE WISDOM DIVINE FROM WITHIN ALL THAT THINK TO ASK, TO HEAR OF THIS THEY SHALL RECEIVE.

FEEL AS THOUGH YOU ARE TO BE IN AN ACCEPTANCE TO LET GO OF ALL THAT IS OLD AND NOT IN NEED. THIS IS THE WAY IN WHICH WE WISH TO EVOKE FROM YOU THE SEEING OF YOU, THE REAL YOU THAT YOU NEED.

In ones asking to see the REAL me it is to be the internal being that desires of this to be so. For to wish to see a better me, a prettier me or a more desirable me, a different me in the physical way in which it is to look is not correct for thee. You are this beautiful devotion from within to be spoken of as it is you to be correct in all that you see. So, to feel as though it is to change the physical of course it can be done but by the holding onto what is not it will never please you to become.

The seeing of self and in this we say is the complete way in which it is that we see you. Perfection in every cell that you be. Imagination needed here to detail the version of you that we see, it is to be filled yet free to flow in her entirety of this that she be. Never holding or feeling the need to be. Senses open to receive in all that she sees limitless to be found from within and the view to be a creating of always more to begin. We offer this vision of you to be realised by the real you that seeks to see. One is often in disregard for the beauty that they are to hold within for many tales and untruths have been spoken to be offered to you the seer in which it is that one is to think or portray what they should be.

Remove all doubt in a blockage as such to be willing to trust this that you are the very real version of self to become. For she is you in a complete sense of which it is to know, You are to be desired by this that you are of for your form holds no pretence into a thought that you have to be. It is only of the mind that holds captive your visions of self to be. Let all that enters ones head to think be asked to be forgiven in a certain way with kindness attached as a belief in this that you aren't, for you will soon begin to notice those changes that you are to have asked. You will develop an innate ability from within to hear not of another but only in your heart this space of total commitment to you to speak of you in this way that you so wished of self to be. Watch as the transformation is to become you in a way, that what you thought to ask or speak of self once upon a time, is not needed by you today. Ones perceptions are always changing it would offer to say to become more in alignment with the heart that speaks to you in this way. If one is to listen to hard truths to hear all day and in every way, then it is of this that the hardened cover of yourself shall offer this to say. But watch as you are to increase your abilities from within to speak to yourself in a very gentle caring way, this is what we see to offer to you to be. You are the realest version of self to be held within, let her speak in this way.

YES, **we hear you say, we all like to look good. Is this not correct?**

One is devoted to the physical earthly image that they are to present to self to see. About this image it is for us to see it upsets the many of you that are to look at it in this non-accepting specific way. To see oneself in a continuance as to not be pleased or unhappy to view of you to be found, one will always feel unsettled into how it is that they are to look no matter the amount of improvements or accessorising that one undertakes. Look deeper within here to correct the words that you utter to say, for these are the most damaging to your body and looks and in you it will hinder the way that you be the true believer of all that you may. See not of yourself in an image of another for they are to look their own certain way, being shown from within is the truth that one must observe to see. You are in this willingness to begin?

I AM THE COURAGE THAT I
LOOK WITH TO SEE ME.

I AM THE BEAUTIFUL THAT RESIDES IN ME.

MY OWN BEAUTY TO LOOK UPON IS
THIS THAT I AM TO SEE.

I AM NOT WILLING TO VIEW ANOTHER
AS MY BEAUTY TO BE.

IN THIS KNOWING TO BE SPOKEN IN
KIND AND HAPPY WORDS, I AM.

I WILL FEEL MY OWN BEAUTY TO
SHINE FROM WITHIN TO COVER &
SATISFY THIS ALL THAT I AM.

WHY, is it that you describe of us in this way?

We see not to see you in any other way. For it is of your unique light that we are witnessed to see. It is not of this hardened structure or form that you have chosen to sit within, for it is of this that is no use to thee. We see you radiating from within to the eternal reaches of all that you shall be. In this desiring to be seeing of another; may we suggest that you are to not. Your self will only rely upon this that you are to think as words to rest within you to be. You are all different in this revealing we agree, but to your own defence you asked of it to be.

See the light that is of one's own uniqueness to shine and it will lead you home to the heart space within that is to hold of you there. Your colours are all extreme in their eagerness to beam. Feel this intent from within that this is the way we see you   instead.

You are the gifted being that has found her/his place here so it is of us to offer that we insist that you feel this intent to rise from within for you are willing and able to be this that you speak. Let yourself feel the security in words that are to come. In one's own uniqueness it is to feel this that they are to be one, for you were all divinely placed into this form that you chose and in this it was of yours to ask for it to be your own. So, see it is to be said that you were the chooser of this identity to be yours.

Now, it is that one should be amazed, that you chose this form as the chosen way to be viewed to live this life and experience it as you. It was you, your soul that was to know of the exactness that you were needing in this one to become.

One's growth is offered in many ways and to be witness to the body of self that you became, ask of it this, **in what has it to share.**

Look beyond the physical to see if one must but in truth if you are to speak to this that you are you will hear to see the feelings and likes of this that you be. Your choice was desired so intensely requested by you, so in this it is to know that you will be this that you are until it is that you become again into another so choosing of you to cherish. It is in only ones physical or the earthly death that you will truly know to express that you so did choose of self to be exactly this correct.

Let us feel free to offer a suggestion to most,

See yourself here in this to hear if you can allow, you chose YOU this being to be, this casing to express, you chose YOU in every way. Of here it is that one should know, you are the expression that desired from within this form to be to undertake this earthly adventure to have begun, in this exactness that you see you knew that this was the ONE that could handle all that needed to be lived into, learned, achieved or accepted to become. Rejoice here into this humanoid image that you see, but know this to see that the loving being in essence that you are is the 'I' that glows so brilliantly from within, an image maybe not yet able for you to see her as this bold that we see, but none the less you are you,

FABULOUS in every way expressed as YOU.

FEEL THE DIFFERENCE THIS SENTENCE IS TO MAKE TO YOUR THOUGHTS OF HOW AND WHY YOU BECAME YOU.

You asked of this willingness to be you and in your wanting of this to become, you did in such a powerful way with intentions in all areas to be this beautiful complete being that we see as you.

Your difference in self to be is just this unsatisfaction of the outside to see, but let us guide you here to say that when one feels the surge of satisfaction and eagerness to arise from within it will shape the exterior to be seen in a new an furthering space to be sitting within this force that you've become.

We see not of you to be all sitting here in doom and gloom.

It is in one's physical eyes that they see only of this human that you be if one is to have this view of self to be then it will present as this to be. You are the doom and gloom that you allow yourself to be felt into as yours to see. We see only light when we look upon you, for your courageous stance that you have stood into to take was yours to become this light to shine in this place that you NOW stand, becoming the one that is you to be.

Rally with any thoughts from within for they are often overlooked by you as a way to simply be, your chance to change in an instance will come and prove to you that it is of you that you can in the words that you are to speak. Let your voice ask strength within to be found for you are not all this doom and gloom no matter how hard you are to be found resistant to this change that we offer here, it must come from only you this that you are within. We speak with a gratitude to you to be offered here in these words to say, Many challenges it feels to see by you that one has to overcome in this life that they have lived to this date to be. In these challenges it is not to hold remorse or doom and gloom attitudes for of what it could have been. You were extravagant in the asking of these to be yours to further your growth and experience this beauty from within to be witness to this self in this position that seems different to most. It is of your own truth, the real truth that you be that you will become and not of another's way to view.

Into you it is that we sit eternally placed for you to be willing to see of us there again in this your time it is to speak of the request to see us within. We sit in a confidence within you to be found upon your asking of this beauty to be felt.

When spirit speaks......

The courageous being within is the contagious way to be, spreading these words of solitude, contentment, and joy from within. She speaks so gallantly of this to me. She offers words to comfort and secure me from within.
Allowing of this I wish to be.
She sees no wrong within this that I am to present and in this I struggle to feel content. For I have looked upon myself in a totally different way of past in which it is that she is to look at me. She is the true seer I am told, and she sees no wrong in all that she has been told.
She boldly speaks of a wisdom that is to run deep, so deep that it has been imprinted upon my soul to keep sacred and contained within to be always of a realising of this great that I became and of this it is that

I AM

Getting REAL with MYSELF

It is of this that I am to hear in words that are offered to me to hear to speak with you. One must be obliging and have a sense of kind willingness to speak on their own behalf, for it is to be said that not many will speak like this to you. Kind words are to become your friends to speak to you, they will build you up and elevate you to become a knowing existence of this that you be the beautiful me that sits within you. You are to not disregard your thoughts of how to for it is a challenge this we see to set in motion from this place that one is to have felt as reminiscing of the real you that you once might of knew. It has been a while it is that we see for the many of you to have felt complete and content in the all that you be. Sense this voice from within to speak as you do, she sounds like you but in kinder truths to be offered to you to be heard. One is to be honest in self for all that you see has been positioned, dumped and offered upon this frame that you see, letting yourself feel neglect and being not interested in this that you have appeared to become. It has felt like eternity to some since they have felt a happiness to succumb to this belief to be totally and full of this to be themselves seen as total-ness and of one. We see the many of you to stand there in this place of non-respect and allowing yourself to be saddened and listening to what seems to be someone else. Let us say that this is to be in exactly of what it was to be heard by you.

Your truth has laid dormant and covered for a while it may seem, getting lost in distractions of others and situations that are to take you away from being able to sit in the silence that one is to crave, to feel, to be this sense of stability within. You must if you are to succeed in this new viewing of you to be not of another but only for you to make a commitment in a heartfelt space of this to be that you will try with all your might to become the speaker of words that you are wishing to hear.

Your words can be tainted with hatred or love feel as both are expressed from this mouth to be yours to speak and you will feel instantly the heaviness from within this you to feel of the words that sit heavy and harshly upon your skin. These words of untruths and misgivings are of remorse, often regret and sadness to be said and felt.

The human body is not responsive it seems to these words from thee. It refuses to shine under these conditions we might say. Let others be held at bay, for if they too feel this unsettledness from within it will be hard for them to offer you words to suit your intent of inner happiness to begin. In the lighter side of voices that speak only of words that shine and raise you up these words filled with encouragement and love are to let you feel like you are to explode from inside. Let these words be your comrades of choice for you, to be there supporting you to recognise this magnificent creature that you BE.

Try as I might, I cannot utter these words to myself to speak.

This statement is to sadden us so. But it is of one that we are to hear of often spoke.

If one is to allow of self to think of us as a thinker like this to be. This we are not. But we do offer here in this that we are that the light that we shine upon all to be they will know of our intent if likened of it to be.

Speak all words as if to be your own, never of another is this to be said. For let us offer, your words are easier to change than of what has been laid upon you by another. Ones words will be willing to change if and only when it is your time to stand into this righteous being of love that you are, **you must want/ask for this.** For it cannot be offered by another. Only you hold this power that is the "I" within you and in this power, you will begin to unfold and see the blooming of someone who will appear to be everything special in her right to be.

HERE I AM to begin...

In this commitment to myself.

I ask of myself to be willing in just this time to provide myself with a selection of words to be wrote or spoke. In these words, I will feel no judgment from myself and I will feel to know they are all worthy to be heard.

....
....
....
....
....
....
....
....
....
....
....
....
....

These words that appear here upon your pages to write are your words to witness as needing to be seen. If they have a hardness surrounding them let it feel content as the action that you spoke of these words to be truths that you needed to hear. For in all the ways in which it is that one is to think; you are constantly being reminded of the judging from within. Words like these are hard to speak for one has often never been receiving of ones such as these. It is to feel this as a step towards the becoming that you shall demand from within to be you to see yourself as all that we speak of you always.

Stand into this space of love to be felt.

For some of you in your trying this may have felt extremely hard to do. For others it will come easy to write. Others we see may not even feel like it was a commitment that they were willing to make. For some you may hesitate to write and not feel this as a need to do. This is okay we say it is all in your being that you know in right for you to do.

Opportunities Abound

There are many opportunities to express words of LOVE to self to hear in many moments of your day. You are to seek out these opportunities to speak kind words of forgiveness and love. Respect of what is to be offered by many that you witness to share the GREAT that you are. You are to look only for the good in the way in which it is that you are to speak. We are witnessing the many ways in which it is to be offered to you upon your planet in materials of study or self-help information to improve your way to view oneself.

Yes, this we say will help you to begin and further your voice to expel unworthy from within. One is to think of this to begin but know that you are the commander of your ship to steer you correct.

Correctness comes from within it is to appear in ways that you are to be conscious to receive. Look for the joyful ways in which you can fill your thoughts or voice into how it is to see yourself to be.

JOY
IS ALWAYS
YOURS TO BE

CHAPTER FIVE

WANTING MORE

FREEDOM TO ALWAYS WANT MORE IS YOURS TO ALWAYS FEEL, IS IT NOT? IN THE EXPANSIVENESS THAT IS TO APPEAR AS LIMITLESS IN ALL THAT IS, IS THE ABILITY THAT ONE MUST SEE INTO TO FEEL AS THOUGH IT IS ALWAYS IN A WILLINGNESS TO BE.

The wanting of more is a basic understanding of the human that looks to always feel to see as though they would like more. Whether this is to rise out of the request for more love, more joy, more money or even just more days to live into this beautiful life that you love. The natural ability within one to think of self as to not have enough leads the individual to think in the thinking mind to see of limitations to all that one has. The view of to feel as though you are not able to see or worthy of to view more of whatever it shall represent to you to see or have is where the undecidedness is to lay and the contradiction to all that is possible to be yours lays.

I want MORE of this that 'I AM'.

To word it like this is incorrect, for you and the all that you are in this being of love to be you: Is always more; ever continual in your flow of success and continuation of this self to be. So, let us say that you are always to be more in this that you are connection wise to these that see you to be always more.

Often in the human way of which it is to see of more is the way that ones such as those that are to ask to feel into the asking of it to be, whether this be in a guilty to ask offering or an attitude towards the thinking that you are not worthy to have more, the deliberate calibration within self to rely on others to offer more to you or to think that they are to owe you this more. It is witnessed by us in many occasions to see into that the thinker within this space that you occupy is to be the provider of thoughts and actions at times to be you the deliberate duller of more to be yours.

In words that are offered by one it is to always expect more, for it is yours and in this entitlement to be thought of as. **It shall.**

SO, you are suggesting that in my words to offer, I will receive MORE.

Why, would it not be yours to think of this to be?

If one is to ask, there is always more.
Is there not?

We are not limited in our viewing of this to be thought, as should you neither. Your worlds as ours are to be the ever provider of more to be. It is the rules of attraction that are to be adhered to in a sense to speak of in the advice of many to have offered these thoughts, ideas and words to speak before.

To feel as though this is not in your vocabulary or ability to express than it shall not be for you to grasp this wonderment of always more to be yours. The deliberate intent within ones such as you and the all that be was to always be of a continuation and flow of correction into the all that is, so in this we mean to offer that to even think of this as of something to concern your thoughts with, is not to be.

It simply just IS.

We are as you to be spoken of here in this to be yours to hear, to feel these words as we speak you are the deliberate creators, the experiencers of self to expand, the wanted to be here in this your now, the love to be shone so brightly from within. So, would you not stop to think of this self as the attractor of all that is to be yours to appreciate in such an honesty of self to be realising of as yours to have.

Create intent from within we say for you are all equipped with this innate ability to be the one that is, and in this way to think of self to be, you will, and you are.

This that is to be the offering into the all that you think of self to be the mindless chit chat that often takes over ones thoughts in the human realm of sensing of self to be is where the dilemma is to lay within to think of self as being worthy or ever in the seeing of more to be theirs.

Is it to think that more always must be materialistic to be seen? It is advantageous within this that you are to live into a world that is so focused upon what it is that you see. To see of the all that is to surround you as to {in this we mean of others so choosing of this more to mean security or flashiness or influential ability} than yes, it is to see more in this way. One is to feel within their own understanding of what is more to them. Would it not be fair to ask of this to you that in the seeing of more in another is to be felt as a resentment in most cases to see the feelings that are to arise from within labelled as jealousy, inadequacy's or an unworthiness in self.

YES, in most cases and this we see concerning the human nature of greed, hierarchy, authority and ability to feel as though it may be a belittling to others to show or display this wealth or abundance than it is to be in NO means thought of as an eager more to require within self to see.

Let us elaborate upon this subject of MORE,

When ones to be are in the human brain to think it is this expression to be thought or expressed that more is to be more, by this we mean why is it that ones to be are to feel that in what they are is not already the 'MORE' to be expressed.

Why is it to limit ones thinking to the restrictive side or ability or lean towards caution to be speaking in self already as MORE. You are if able and willing to eliminate these thoughts to be more completely for just in these words to be felt to be spoken, you are an admittance within self to be of NOT, Is this not correct to ask?

YOU ARE ALWAYS MORE.

To want more has feelings of GREED, GUILT even UNWORTHINESS attached to it for ME, shouldn't I be happy with what I already have?

Why would one associate feelings of these to the ability to always want more, more is not to be viewed in the eyes of one that will not share or to be on display of this wealth or more-ness that they appear to have. To think of another in this way is the evidence that one needs to see within themselves of the resentment that lays often deeply within to be happy for others in this position of more in abundance in all areas of one's life to live. It is in the thinking mind to feel this within self and in these thoughts to be one must not. All that present to you are in their choosing of this to be theirs and in your ability to feel just love and a satisfaction within self you will eliminate any feelings of dread or regret to allow more to be yours to.

In ones open and consolable heart to witness you will feel of a genuine ability to be revealed to you the seer to only want for the wellbeing and happiness to be of those that you are to witness as to have more than you have. To think of it in this way serves your sense of completeness within you to be willing to feel joy for another, not jealousy.

NOTE:

Feel into yourself as we offer the word in your language to speak THINK... it is a big word that carries many suggestions and appears to contain a lot of thought around it. Does it not? THINK is to be thoughtful or to express oneself in words to speak, mindful thinking, words in your head, to read too much into one's thoughts, ideas, overthinking, free thoughts.

In one's ability, one should observe their thinking in how it is they think. This then will help elevate the thinking process to become one that serves in love and kind, and not of one that diminishes thy self.

We see the many of you to experience moments of wanting to feel responsive into as to entice or complete you to be the real reasoning behind the asking of more. Is this correct?

Seeing self without is detrimental to the loving being that you are to experience as you in only the way to see oneself to be, fulfilled and complete in this YOU, you are.

'In more there always is' we say.

It is all within you to see this of yourselves to experience. In this we wish to offer that one is more and is always in difference to another's. Let all feelings of not to have as this that another is or of to be allowed to be put to rest by asking yourself in this your now.

<u>Is this of what I really think to be my more?</u>

For we can guarantee that all that you see to be more, is most often not your version of more....

Sense into one's way to feel around this subject that we speak to find this that you feel comfortable within to feel regarding MORE.

'MORE' Is misleading it seems in the word offered.

Why would one not want to think of this to be so? to be more.

Be expansive within oneself to think of their own 'MORE' and the words of attraction to surround you as to the more that you are entitled to have.

MORE does not need to have a negative attachment to it if it is spoken of in a way that suits you.

Find the meaning of more to you; to think.

Is it generous or giving, loving & full,
or thankful, allowing, gathering,
seeing, humble, drawing, attracting,
blessed, we have many ways to express
the word more for you to hear?

Let your words represent this feeling of divineness within you to be entitled to all the ways that are yours to cherish self into receiving and always seeing the all that they are to be.

Is it not to offer to ones such a yourself to think that you deserve more love, more happiness, more pleasure, more sex, more contentment, more joy, more motivation, more discipline, more freedom, more challenges, more growth, more holidays, more money, more lovers, more friends, more, more, more.

It is correct to want more; it is to ask with intention of self to realise that this is for you to have. You are the qualifier within self to be, you are the thinker of this self, you are the offeror of this more to be yours. Let your thoughts be not attached to the labelling of more items to be in wanting of, but to feel a deep sense of satisfaction within oneself to know that you are being the true you that you came here to be. You are the true speaker of this self. To be allowing of the voice of truth within to be your speaker, your guider into this that you are to become. She knows of all that you are entitled to in the want to see more and it is this that you are to feel like you are always more in the way in which it is to see not only yourself but others and this life that you live into.

Eternally More

In these words to be offered; it is in our knowing that you will hear them as they are to be spoken to be received.

You are many in this that you are and in this we offer to you to say that you are to be seen in the many ways that you are to be presented to us in the abilities that you are to possess. We sense the greatness and power within you all in all that is to be of you to be. We see this that you are to have become and in this you surely will be eternally more in the eyes of the all that we are the willingness, the wanting within you to feel of us to be. See internally of the all that you hold within for she/he is to always be a greater part of this eternalness that we speak so boldly of, for it is this way to be that one must live into this constitution that they so have chosen to become, for there is always more and it is part of the human 'spirit' shall we say, the greater good that lives within you all to present here to us to ask of that you will ever be eternally more in this greatness that is ours to see.

WHY WAIT WE ASK; TO BE MORE IS YOURS

We want this for you, for this to be your hearing of this decision to be more.

This more is so intently held within, stop to listen to the words of great that are spoke by your innerness, your soul, your love for you in the words that she/he are to speak. Can you hear this to be expressed from within? Let one's inability to hear or the limited thinking that they cannot, be allowed to be forgiven. In this we are to offer; it is in most that we see are trying to hard.

What is it that you are wanting?

We are often to say to this host that she be to ask herself in her times of connection.

The want to be more is offered with hard feelings attached this we notice, but in the allowing of oneself to sit into a quiet place of reserve within self to feel as an intent from within to be heard this we offer, you shall.

Authors experience to share: MORE has not always been easy for me to see, let alone accepted by me.

In my diligence from within to be respecting of all that I have had and have NOW, I was always of this to express that I have all that I need and happy to stay here where it is if I may. Feeling grateful and humble to have what I have, too scared to dare ask for MORE. I have lived a life filled with happiness and love to be expressed, have I not? I ask myself this to be expressed in all that I speak. I felt disturbed in angst to feel like it was to be mine to express in as more to be displayed or craved. This is the way is it not? or so I thought to be in the spirt of love and grace. This I was to feel expressed deeply from within my response from these that guide me in my every way, day to day moment of self to reflect I heard this to be offered my way.

As you will too feel yours expressed correct for you.

In ones hearing from others and a young age, I often heard spoken words such as these; YOU always want More, you are never happy with what it is that you have, nothing is ever good enough for you, is it?, why cant you just be happy with what you have?.....etc (sound familiar? maybe you have experienced the same conversations or been on the receiving end of similar statements) these words of contempt even harm I will express them to be to me now have obviously sat deep within my psyche to be expressed, yet also hidden away. Your stories of truth I'm sure to be told by you will unravel and in this I am encouraged to tell that they will, expressions or comments of contempt and disregard, unjust and disrupt are all heard whether young or old, in situations and stages of your earthly life, present within they are to rise perhaps again in a remembrance or offering as mine were presented for me to observe.

In the memories of past gone by, young that I was an impression was left. Have I lived with this in my shadow of self to be thinking that to ask of or to have MORE was totally wrong? YES, I now can answer this as correct. I asked to spirit or my intuitive guide to answer my query of this to be made, You are the believer of most where you not?, you were to be a hearer to think that they {and in this we are to offer family, friends, lovers, yourself included, even strangers} to offer words, comments and instances to be laid deeply within you to be held or attached to this self that you be unwillingly it would seem non-coherent to this innocent or even unknowing attack that has been embedded within, living silently almost undetected whether by choice or oblivious to be felt, to be expressed, no memory or recall maybe to appear in the human that you are or have become. But certainly, shaping deceivingly so without one's ability to know of or even remember it to be there. Let oneself feel free here to express, ask directness in love to be spoken here by oneself to the seer within that is the real you.

Please ask of this statement, words or memory in an acknowledgment of it to be discovered to be released from your thoughts even better your form, ask for it to be detached and seen as not of yours to require any longer to be yours. All negativity is felt so deeply unaware within, often in disguise offered by a loved one to have said.

I ask {if you were in the right space or frame of mind to ignore even} tender of age you were not able to distinguish words that were spoke as whether right or wrong, in the use of words such as these or did you tuck them away and live into them every day. Crystal clear it may appear to you now, to see that you did not know of the damage that was and would be done. I felt compelled to disclose this revealing side from within this human that I be that in all of my asking I have come to be, this that I am and I am accepting of this ME but more importantly I am forgiving of ME, for not seeing this as not needed by me. So, in this NOW that I am free to speak, I see myself worthy of MORE as a continually trying to acknowledge this as a grand willingness to be. Here in this ME that I be, I stand willing to accept this as WHO it is that I AM. It is this that I suggest and you either will or not in your time, leave off all that you feel attached by another's thoughts, suggestions or comments to be spoken, even if to think that love was their initial intent for maybe not so and it is in this that we offer you are the changer here in this space, <u>to let it all go.</u>

If not straight away but it will rise from within you in this sense of satisfaction to be called ours to be heard, to be felt, to be wanted, to be yours to sit into. It is then you will be a knower of this to be heard as your voice of stability, your presence that sits within to be heard for you are just tuned to a different frequency we would offer to you to think of this that we be. You are often deafened within self and the world that is to surround you dulls down the interpretation that one must feel to hear what is already within. He/she is your voice of love, your voice of truth, your light that shines bright for all to see. Let this need to be more be as extravagant as it needs to present to you to be, you will be the determiner of what more is to mean to you. Hold it not in comparison of this more to be of another's for they too are searching it seems to find in one's ability to feel of what more means to them and the meaning of more in relation to what it is that they are to have.

A sense of gratitude, satisfaction, bliss and happiness is to overwhelm you at times to witness yourself in the deliberate creation of this more to rise within you to feel in many ways to be offered to you. You will feel this to create an urging for more to be yours to feel and see into. Embrace these feelings of more, of completeness, to sit into a time of nonchalant to be, a quietness to explode from within for in these moments of which it is to witness yourself sitting into is to allow for these to be the leaders of your thoughts to know that you are truly worthy and deserving of more.

We ask you…. Why shall you not be MORE?

CHAPTER SIX

My ABILITY TO SEE MORE

ONE'S ABILITY TO SEE MORE WITHIN SHALL WE SAY IN CORRECTION OF IT TO BE IT WOULD BE BETTER OFFERED AS TO BE ETERNALLY VIEWING OF THIS FOCUS TO BE ALWAYS MORE.

In ones attention within self to be held here into this that one thinks to be their only now to be present within one would find to feel that this more that they speak of is to be a suggestion by self's thoughts to be only of what it appears that one can think of themselves to be thinking of more as it shall be for them.
Is this not correct to ask?

In ones desiring of this ability within oneself to be improved or shall we say to offer that one can resist the common approach to thinking of more to be on a practical side rather than to be in a position of well within to simply pull to receive of this more in a knowing that you automatically are attracting more and always will be.

The sense of stabilisation around one's persona shall we say in character or reference to this personality that you are to think of self to be.   Yes, this we offer that the limitations attached to this form to think is in the possibility of which it is that you would hold yourselves into.

So how do I or would I free myself from this stagnant thinking?

One would in just this question to ask feel the sensation to be trapped in a way to think of themselves to be or see themselves as:
Would they not?

So, to comprehend this ability,˝ this inner knowing˝ of self to evolve and to naturally crave or require more is to set down all reservations that one might have or may carry within this head of yours to think as the thinker within to be your controller to think of it as this. To allow for this we say to speak to you to grasp that in one's thoughts to think of this more to be or not an option, **it shall be.**

We sense a willingness into a vulnerability that is pronounced louder in one's thoughts to think of this as a scenario into to receive, for this as a new way in which it is to think, Should we not?

I AM WILLING to take on this new concept of MORE to mean, YES.

In this space of an idea that is to be presented as a new concept one would word it as, it is to be your thinking of self to be willing to be open to or less resistant to another availability to you to see into. To take on another opinion or view within self to see is to evaluate your interaction within self as to the ways in which it was of you to think regarding this subject to be expressed within you.

Why, would it not be of benefit to you in this understanding to realise of the ability or sensing of more to be attainable for you. It is always in the reasoning mind that one feels to sense a lack of, even in the eyes that view from the physical mind's perspective are often clouded by a sensing or reality of this to be all that is.

How would I change MY view then to see MORE?

We say, one is to ask are they not?

To be seeing of what is practical and every day to view is often hard on the imagination or meditative states of self to want to see into as a perception of this reality as it would appear to be. So, in this we advise one to close your eyes to look into oneself as to be always of more than they could fathom this human self to be. For often it is not in the seeing so much that one must change but rather the view in change of opinion as to what it is that more is to you in its availability to be offered to you to see. In this sense of self to be willing to alter their state of perception into ones thoughts of more they will be enticed by the newest direction of correction to witness into to see inwardly to become of this more to be theirs, knowingly as a new found ability to progress into as a request from the divine self within to offer this to you. For you are of this divinity that we speak to be delivering to this version of you to be in a place of which it would appear to be in the receiving of the all that you are as one would put it; entitled to have. Is it not this to speak into?

One must be accepting of this notion within self to be a divine intervention of this human that you are to present as simply just the holder of this that you truly are and in this acceptance often lays doubt and inhibitions to be formed by you interacting along this so life that you have chosen into, Yes we say it is in the learning and challenging periods at times but they are all to venture with you to be explored outwardly in a place of which it is to observe from to view it as an experience.

We sense of this willingness within to ask, well how do I wrap my head around these comments or statements offered to make this new way of thinking work for me?

IN this we feel to respond to you, WHY WOULD IT NOT?

To think that it would not or that one cannot is the true underlayer here in one's power of thought to be the receiver of this question to be asked.

You as the challenger to self to be fighting with, is the minds view or inhibitions of this reality that you see yourself in to, to think in this way do you not?

We feel to get through to you one must take the thinking ability away from this subject, to just allow for all that is to be yours in the more it naturally already is. Spoken to hear, the easier, or gentler the approach or viewing of more that one has; the less resistance that one will feel towards this subject of MORE, in turn allowing for more to always be more than of what one thinks it shall.

So, are you suggesting here that I have been blocking MORE TO BE MINE?

In a simple answer YES, it would appear to be seen this way. When one is resistant to thoughts or projections shall we offer here to be this that you are not, than one will only feel to be focused into this certain spot, place or thought to think into, shall they not?

So, to understand this way of which it is to acknowledge that more is you. It is for you to view of it internally first not in a way that it is to be a something or someone of which to have to hold, for it is not. You are to be willing in your placement of thought to just allow for all to flow and to know that you are the manifestor of always more to entice you, to will you, to propel you, to extend you in a certain aspect of this magnificent self to be.

You SPEAK OF MORE as GOOD, but can it also be not so great?

YES, this we would offer as a great question to ask into.

When one is to be a thinker of sorts to say in this ability it lays in the power of one's thoughts that are so impressionable to become a reality or a sense of to be. Does it not?

So, in this yes, it is to say that the MORE of anything to think shall be. It is really this simple to offer to you to hear. That in this we speak has been offered in many conversations both with this channel and many, many more who have interpreted this message in this to be offered.

"In the seeing it shall always be"

Let us elaborate, in this existence [you] to be seen to be the asker of MORE, it shall. So, to respect of all that you ask to us to represent it shall. We are not the determiners that lay so profusely and willingly within to be the hearers, the offerors, the knowers of all that you desire. It is in our entirety to speak that we are the entireness that you desire of us to be known to you once again in your ever-ness to become to be again infinite to see.

The true asker is careful it is to be told that more is always offered in the preferred way in which it is that the speaker is to ask of it to be.

What is it that you see prevalent around you?

Is it the life that you are asking for{we determine not as bad or good, easy or hard for you are the asker} are you not portraying to the outer-ness that you are to be the seer of all that you be, do and have.

In ones thought of this to be ever so powerful in their comprehension of this to be theirs to sit into. One will begin to realise that they are the creator, the manifestor, the producer or director of this so-called movie or play that you are to participate into as yours to learn and experience into. So, to feel the pretence that is associated with to want more is to be general in your thinking of more to be simply an asking to grow, to expand, to experience of this that you think into; is it not?

Think to be just this more in an ease of sensing this to be a willingness in you to always want to ask for more, more in a great way, a bold way, a loving way to be expressed through you as an understanding that you will always be more of this that we are in its entirety of it to be seen as yours.

What if I AM unable TO SEE THIS AS CORRECT WITHIN me?

Then this would be offered here to you to hear that it is always correct in its placement or viewing of you to see into, Is it not?

In one's ability to think outside of themselves and in this we say outside of the regimented thinking mind to present to you regulations and rules to sit into a conformity of self to be held into, then one must start to negate the real possibilities that are always presented to them in thoughts to be or not.

So, would it not be beneficial to assume the way to think of as I'm more to be the ruler let's say to one's opinion into this that they can see as a better more pleasing option to think.

We do not choose this way for you to think that you do, you are the decider in many thoughts of self to be often being guided here into this space of holding to be offered to you by thoughts that sit within others conversations, suggestions, ideas or offerings to you to be hearing into.

So, negate most of what it is that you are to hear offered, to be left to them to be theirs to know as their own truths and let your truths within become yours to view to know of as the way in which it is to understand your deciding of this that you are to see always more within you to be yours in the correct way for you to always be MORE.

CHAPTER SEVEN

IN THE MORE-NESS THAT YOU ARE

TO FEEL OF THIS CALIBRATION FROM WITHIN TO BE YOURS IN A SENSE AS A CONFIGURATION OF WILLINGNESS TO RECEIVE, TO KNOW THAT YOU ARE DESERVING OF ALWAYS MORE.

One must be in a certain willingness shall we say to experience life as it is to appear before you to witness into an ability to present to self to be of an example of let's say a magnet that is magnetised to the attraction of like-minded thoughts and people to presume it is of this that you are envisioning to become.

For to be energised from within into this ability to see self as a confident attractor to the creations of your so desiring of thoughts in them to be, you shall. One is to eliminate all hinderances from the thinker to be allowing of one to clear or open space to let nothing sit into it other than a pureness of nothingness to be calibrated within you to feel a sense not to need.

Know in a deliberate asking of this self to want or ask to be more is most often, if not always attached to a suggestion from the speaker to ask of it to be titled or so named. Let all these formalities as we would express them to be as not needed here in this now of yours to ask of to feel rising from within to think of self to require. You are the sensing within ones experience to know of the formatting that you are contained into is a denser version of us shall we say and in this insistent need to be more in a human expression of it to be spoken it will always feel to you as a lack from within in regards to the what I have and what I don't, and what I think I need.

Feel an ease of release wash over you in this to experience within self in any given moment of your time to be relieved in a sense to not see of self as to want, need or ask more. For just in the non-descript intention that is to lay within you in the initial feeling to say of it to be felt as a request, image or idea even as to the furthering of your thoughts surrounding more; you are to know that you will.

No thing or body are to be coherent into any other state other than to be a manifestation within itself to be evolved in to. So, in this we say that all that is to be thought of as to be a general sensing of more to be, will. The asker and the asking are often contained within a distraction to say that this is of what it is that I must have, be or do.
IS IT NOT?

So, often it is for us to offer this new information to you to hear into that it is just as it is to be. Just this SIMPLE. The fearing to not be enough or not have enough to repeat is to damage the clear intentions of self to be in charge shall we say of what it is to be more for you. You are entitled to this and the whole of all of humanity plus more of further existence within self to be even able to think of. So to establish a ground base understanding here for you to resonate; one must be accepting of self to be in this satisfaction, completeness or loving ability to see of only this that they are to be the more in its entirety to be this that we hold within us to be seen into.

We shower all this loving energy upon you in this form to interpret as this that we are and in this it is to always feel the sense of freedom within to rise up to be in a place of such contentment to be this that you are and to be absolute in comfortability of self to be. IS IT NOT?

Here to offer, why would you trouble your thinker self to suggest another option to dwell into as a need to be thinking of more in a way that is not to be seen as successful to you to inherit these or encourage these already innate abilities to see this more of you that you are always in a truth to be.

One is to falter into a state of regretting when they are combatted or confronted with an opposing position within another to offer this to you to think that you are not of this to be your more. Seek not to be an avid listener to be of any concern to be a requiring of this to be thought of or seen as a suggestion for you to be equipped into.

One is to remember here in this that is a coherent state of which it is to understand into; that you are always of more to evolve out of this that you are to become of in the engrained originality that one is to be naturally gifted from the source component, the power, the force of the all that be you to speak of to be always MORE to see.

I am withdrawing all limitations regarding more to be not for me.

We are to offer this here as a statement of truth to feel within this form that you are to feel it settle deeper within your cognitive state of which it would be to think of this as a confirming or positive statement to be for you to realise the greatest potential that is to lay within this that you are the hearer of all that is magic to lay within.

You are always more.

See this in ones sensing of self to know for often it is held in a self-denial shall we say as a prospect to allow one to think that they are worthy to be receiving of more, do not doubt the power of the restricted mind here to believe in the suggesting by others to say that one must not ask of more to be theirs to see this as an insult to all that appear not to have or be.

In this we offer this suggestion to explain this to be in their thinking of not to be they shall. It is a forgiveness within oneself that we are to display to all that are to inhabit or interact into this presuming of this life that they are to lead as to not have. But we are to wish here for you to accept that one is to never presume upon an initial look or over one's current situation to be presented to say that they do not nor will they ever have.

One is to see all of this that they be to be a contract within themselves and into this life that they are living into as this experience of self to be the willingness that has come to believe into this that they are to assume of themselves to be.

One is always willing to interpret their words of this that they speak as an inner knowing of this self to speak in a certain knowing truth from within to predict the forecast of what it is that one is to see themselves into. Let the words from one's mouth or voice be always to feel of an encouragement to be forthcoming to hear, to feel as this the trueness within you that one must deliver to self to hear in all moments of this existence to be theirs.

I believe you in this you speak, but it sure is hard to implement into my human life.

It is often hard to stay connected into these thoughts of self to be positive and in alignment with the truth that is to be yours. Is this not correct to ask?

You are the decider of this we have spoken. You are the receiver to be this that you ask of, feel into all thoughts and suggestions of self to be allowing to sit intentionally within this that you are as correct into your way of which it is to think of yourself to be complete. The flow of these words to self to hear will get more intentional and determined within one to feel this we are to say in a polite correctness to be heard. Feel not to be daunted by of what is to initially rise for often one is caught in the concept of unwillingness to be an offeror of good news and to feel great within self to be accepted. You are to always assess those that are to be presenting to you in this frame of mind that appears not to suit your thoughts of self to be. So, in this one must be diligent to think this that they are.

Let us say "ALWAYS MORE"

Authors feelings to share,

I have always been if I am to speak my truth of this to feel within myself of as to not of a want to ask for more to be received in this I as you are to recognise. No doubt you have been exposed to these ideals originating from interaction with family members, friends or certain mobilities or religious structures to suggest that one is to not want for more. Words surround this offering for me that upon the revealing of this chapter to be received to write into I felt of this intent within me to want to know more regarding the thinking of more to be possible. I am often asked; what it is that you are wanting? And in this I have spoken in great detail previously that I felt unworthy, guilty to want more when there are others that don't or even more truthful to be spoke of as not to know of what it was that I should ask for, YES, I attached feelings of greed, not worthy and a self-sabotaging attitude that served me well into my thoughts to think that if I don't have it then it was to my own demise to think of myself as to want it anyway. One such as me would not and could not be worthy to receive more. This sense of to not ask or think of myself to be more was imprinted in my thinking to be of what it was that I interpreted to see and be hearing of in these thoughts for me to hear.

For it was to see myself as content??? Happy??? Fulfilled?? Satisfied???
WAS IT NOT, I NEEDED TO ASK.

In my determination to sit into this offering as such that it was to rise out of myself hearing it honestly revealed, I realised this that I hope you will feel maybe a slight persuasion from within to be to suggest that we are all entitled more, and of this we are worthy to hear this spoken as ours to receive into. Let what of this to suit you, align with your thinking of self to feel of this statement or chapter to be a willingness within this that you are to be accepting of this entitlement that you are more in the more that you are and the way in which it is that you are to focus upon your decision to be accepting of this to be or not.

One is to always be the thinker of this to be held within. So, in this it is to see always more of the all that I see myself to view of and in this I am to endeavour to always feel encouraged and observing of my responses, to always remind myself, to always speak in this that I am. To know that the entitlement of this more to be mine is as such an imagery, yet totally believable suggestion of this to be me.

One is to always be knowing of the deliberate intent that one is to create from within for it is in the forming of this self to be seen as to be the ever expanding soul, the heart keeper, the voice of all, the divine intention within, {however it is you see, or title us as} And it is to be sought by you to think of self as to be the querier, the asker, the seer, the truth speaker to be offering these words of encouragement in a righteousness to be yours to hear.

GO FOR IT WE SAY, STOP HOLDING ONESELF BACK. TIME TO TAKE CHARGE AND BELIEVE IN THIS WONDEFFUL BEING OF MORE THAT YOU ARE.

DO YOU ACCEPT THIS QUEST?

CHAPTER EIGHT

MORE, MORE, MORE.

WE SEE YOU ALWAYS SHINING BRIGHTLY
IN THIS MORE-NESS THAT YOU ARE.

IN THIS WE MAY SUGGEST TO YOU TO ALWAYS
ASK OF MORE, FOR THERE ARE NO LIMITS
UPON THIS THAT IS YOURS TO ASK.

IN MORE THERE IS TO BE ALWAYS AN
EXPECTATION FOR ONE TO FEEL INTO THAT
THERE WILL BE MORE OF WHAT IT IS THAT
ONE IS TO SEE, EXPECT OR HAVE.

IN MORE ALLOWS FOR AN EXPECTATION TO BE
GRANTED GREAT RECEIVING SO THAT ONE CAN
FEEL AS TO NOT LACK OR BE WITHOUT.

Why not ask for more we say?

It is to be seen in eyes of some that to be wanting of more is to be an indecision to some as to why or of what more is to represent to them?

Let yourself always to feel of more not in a scarcity or rarity for it will be seen to be this that the more that there is, is to only encourage more of such to be available. It is not to see oneself as without for to be ever receiving one must be genuine in their thoughts of themselves to be ever more, full and abundant in all ability to receive into this way to think.

It is of this that we wish to offer that in this one (you), one is receiving ever eternally this more to become so in this we say that there is no end or completion to be seen to know, so would it not make sense to know that you are to be the all receiver of ever more.

SO MORE, MORE, MORE I SHALL ASK.

In all of humanity and those that exist outside this existence as such to not see into; one is to feel the overabundance to surround oneself in all that they are to look at.

Can one feel this to know that the more that one is to have and feel the pleasure in this receiving they will be in the ability to share to give, to offer with such a gracious heart attached to those that they are to see and to share their more-ness with.

More is not to be perceived as greedy, selfish or only attainable by a certain few. It is in ones understanding of themselves to be that you are to be in the knowing of to right yourself with the satisfaction of that you are always to be a receiver of more in a pleasant way in which it appears to be forthcoming to see or feel.

So much uncertainty upon this planet, lays within countries, societies, family units and especially within the human self and it is driven by the overseers of this that are to be governing your thoughts as to what is a scarcity, or hidden scripture or rare as in a secret sacred to behold by only a few or of something that is not to be available to all to be entitled to. Let your walls of resistance to not enough or not worthy of or even limited regarding ones thinking of this as an issue to be seen as to dissipate.

It is often of those that appear to be in charge of your certainness or express authority to rule/ or impress their power over another to be, in as an expectance by another to accept that ones will falter in their own righteous thinking to know that they are just as worthy and equal in willing to own or express in any given moment to allow for the internal thoughts and words offered to hear spoken to be changed regarding of what it is that you see and in how it is to appear to be.

We sense your hesitation to ask of those that are genuinely living with a sense of scarcity and without.

In this we are to genuinely offer that all are as they are to think themselves to be. Allow the feeling of generosity to become an offering to self in the humanity that is to be of your surrounds, people and countries and your earth to be allowing of this to be seen by all in an entirety of what it is that the real earth should be.

For in the want to see dictators, rulers and leaders to be the offerors of what it is that one is to think has led to the opinions of many to be thought as theirs to be seen in one's opinion and words be those that many have chosen to speak as their thoughts to think into more to be or not for them.

In love to be the powerful offeror it is that one must feel to sit to acknowledge the greatness that is readily available in this to be the human form to sense, the brave, bold, open caring heart of theirs that is to carry with it a natural expectation for all to be of this love and in this to be allowed to share and be bestowed upon all. One will find that in the many that have discovered this real love and are to speak of to spread this word with a sense of complete awareness to the all that are will feel of this moreness to become deliberate in ones attention of it to be always just as this world and the many inhabitants were meant to be in their willingness to see it as theirs.

In human urges to be drawn into a focused intent upon of what is not right or incorrect or horrors to witness, we say that intent focused upon of what is seen will grow in great proportion, will it not?

IN all that is witnessed, it truly IS.

More is to be always in ones asking of themselves first to be felt as a more in an openness from within in just this one simple question to ask that you be seen into the all that you are as the real god inspired version of self to be. Know that this will encourage a great transformation from within to be felt as to the recognising of this love to overflow from this being that you are to be witnessed by the many that interpret you to see, to hear and to witness as this loving being of love that is to participate into this life with such joy, excitement, love and abundance to be shown by you as this that you speak of.

In this simple change to perceive within oneself one will be hesitant to notice of scarcity and not enough to be of them and it will be always in the eyes of love that one will see to experience this world to be.

Let their more-ness be the reason that you are to want to see to change your view, to change the earths peoples view of not only all that this planet holds upon its willing surface but to the many if not all inhabitants that are to grace this beautiful divineness that is offered to you all to live upon.

What would you as spirit describe MORE to represent in you?

We ask in this word to be felt as a completeness within oneself as to ask for an answer than would you not be willing to feel to ask to see that in you, you are complete and there is no lack or not enough of.

We see nothing to be amiss within this that you present to us to see witness to you.

We see all that we be ever expanding into this to grow, learn and to experience so for us it is to be always in more that we see. There is no word here for us to speak into that would suggest a lack of.

More is one's entitlement to be ever becoming always and ones such as us are to be always felt more into the all that we be and surround ourselves in this love that is to fill everything that we see. So in more we are to know this is ours to cherish oneself into as an acceptance of the gracious hearts that we are to vibrate into in a willingness to never speak to see of ourselves as anything less than perfection or love complete.

I AM WILLING to see through your eyes this MORE for me. How shall I begin?

Be of bold in your voice to speak these words of love, to feel this change within you that you are craving from within to not only feel but to see to surround you with an acceptance of perfection that is to be seen within the all that you are present into. Let your thoughts be the change that you are craving and willing to become a part of. In one's own actions firstly to be of this more-ness in a loving embrace to be felt by self it will surely rub off shall we say to the many that are to come your way or cross your path in everyday occurrences. You are the one that must be the change to see in first yourself with kind intentions to be thought and love in heart to be felt words of genuine acceptance of this that you are and then slowly we say for it is a big change that is needed if to be thought of the all that one is to try to do. Let yours be the change that you see to witness as complete within and you will feel the encouragement from those that support and witness to see you as this that they are to see.

WE ARE ALWAYS MORE, AS ARE YOU

In this one voice that speaks these truths for all to hear one will feel the presence of a calmness to evoke within oneself as sense of peace and a calming satisfaction to see this that you are to sit into. It is to be felt here in this to describe as a completeness or certainty that you are to partake into to be the believer of self to be safe and secure. In the ability to not see of self as to be without you will feel the presence of to describe this as us within you. We are to be the true seers that you are to look outwardly through to recognise not only yourself but all that you are to be entertained by to see. In us we offer no suggestion of which it is to speak of not enough or a fear in a sensing of this word to be yours to express.

> WE ARE DELIBERATE IN OUR CREATION OR ATTRACTION TO US OF THIS THAT WE ARE IN A WANTING TO BECOME AS ARE YOU TO KNOW OF THIS TO BE YOURS.

You are to seek so deniably outwardly or external from the self that is held so divinely from within by love to see oneself as and in this often in a confusion as to of what is appropriate to witness for one's own deliberate understanding as to be theirs to trust into. Many as we see of it to be are often led astray by being too focused upon of what is and what isn't, offered by the many that are to present their scenarios or stories to be told to you in a deliberate attempt to be heard by you as of importance for you to interpret your thoughts of these suggestions as yours to sit within. Let all aspects of the thinker within be able to be clear of interpretations, words or emotions to offer to one as they are to speak and to know of this that we say;

IT IS IN THEIR OWN DOING OF A RIGHTNESS WITHIN THEM THAT THEY FEEL TO DO SO.

We are the deliberate creators of this love that we are and in this intense knowing from within it would appear to offer for our circumstance is to be ever free from constraints as to the way in a freedom of to speak as willingness that one is to think. We see of all that sit into this reality that be yours to see as the receivers of many to be interpreted as their own choice of words. YES! we offer, to learn one is to feel as to be in this situation to listen, but the depth of your desire to learn into this that you are to be ultimately is instilled deeply within guiding and enticing you to be felt to follow or pursue into a certain direction as such to be revealed to you as your path of this life to be presented to your knowing.

We see many of you craving this more, do we not.

And in this we are to offer to simply be willing to see through your physical eyes as a not to bombard oneself with words that are to make one feel incomplete which yes granted is hard to do in the situations or circumstance that are to arise for you in this humane challenge it appears to be to live into. If one is willing to utter, speak or even be of a willingness to disregard the ever strong intent from within this mind of theirs to think to speak to be always volunteering falseness in regards to how it is to feel or think or even project into of what it shall become or be. You will feel liberated to express new thoughts and feelings as yours to ask.

The space that is ours to be as yours it is of too. One is in need of this space to be allowing to be felt within as a clarity or sensing of not in need to be filled with needless suggestions of self to be hearing into. Let this space be an emptiness within to be contained by not thoughts or feelings or even emotions as such that one is upon this receiving are to think into.

We are to offer here yes easier said than done, but in the old saying practise makes perfect it certainly goes a long way to help with the change that one is to be looking for to become complete within oneself to be seen.

CHAPTER NINE

SHINING BRIGHT

NOT TO FEEL LIKE YOU ARE SHINING BRIGHT
OR TO EVEN IMAGINE YOURSELF TO
FEEL LIKE YOU CAN OR COULD OR EVER
HAVE... WE OFFER THIS TO SPEAK.

To be balancing an unequalness from within regarding the wholeness that one is to appear to be. If one is to be out of balance shall we say one will feel as to be deterred or aggravated, even a sensing of self to be insufficient about feeling in what it is to want to know to be them.

Ones thoughts become distracted, painful, incomplete or are filled with dominate thoughts as such not to be willing to live into this space that they are to be. In this we offer that one's characteristics are defined within them in the voice that is the speaker to them to hear, whether and in most cases this voice is heard as your physical voice that is attached to the mind that is heavily implemented with woes, worries and contradiction's often of another's to think of as yours to worry over and not of the hearts true presence within to speak of love.

In the justification of all that is to be received by these ears of human existence to which is your hearing ability to interpret of what it is that one is negotiating within to hear as the choosing of words to correspond into. We see many of you left empty or shoved down in a sense to be the receiver of these words as not to help your attitudes or suggestions within self to be thought of as a fulfilment.

One must be in the space of certain alignment we would offer here to think of oneself in and in this we mean to be in a position of which one is to feel joy, inner peace, calm and okay to disregard these words that are harmful in ones thoughts to be needed as worthy to be heard.

We dwell often in this message to be spoken to be received in the many of you that are to carry such heaviness within oneself to be not in an allowance of one to be seen in this way as to offer shall we say light or bright. The brightness that you are that we are privileged to always feel extruding from within to surround you in this greatness to be that you are is our response from within this that we speak to never feel the need to see of you in any other way.

Your shine or light as it would be offered here to feel yourself encompassed by and held so loving within is for you to feel uniquely yours to be blessed and cherished from within it to be felt. One is shining in a continual growth of expansion in many varied hues of intra-fractured beams of colours to be interpreted as yours to see oneself as the originalness that you became. We see many variances of colours of you to be inhabiting to shine in ones learnings or accepting and even speech to feel compelled to be at oneness with this that is to be seen as the one true source of your power within one such as us are to be ever present in this formatting of you to be a willing chameleon shall we say for suggestion as to the ability that one's upon this earth have within them as a truth to speak of the all that they are to become into.

Let your colour filled hues or rays shine from within to the far reaches of this element that we are witness to your deliberate wanting to become of this magnificent hue to be offered here as yours in so choosing of it to be discovered once more. We are all contained within a certain initiation of self to have wanted in this space of becoming and in this it was yours to decide upon this that you did.

Let all inhibitions be dissolved here and forgiven as to being not of a mistake or disagreement within for all was undertaken by you in this form to be a recognition from self to be a willingness to stand here in this that you are to be speaking to hear. Your ingenious ability within this to present is in such a magnificent way to be offered to this form to become that the light that is ever prominent from within is to shine to the heavens and above in the pureness that you are to exist into as you.

We see many rays of enablement to be an asset to this human that you are and love to encourage you upon your receiving from within to be hearing of this magnificence that you were meant to be seeing yourself and others as.

In our thoughts or reminiscing's of you to be always found as this unique creature to be in a want to be ever felt amongst us as this star or ray of light that is to shine ever bright. We ask to never let either you or another dull this light of yours that you are to shine in a willingness to be always interpreted as yours to see. In your own unique pattern of formation, it is to appear as a difference from within this that you be to what of which it is that we see.

One in their own choosing of self to become has established this inter-directness within to be enabled in the so choosing of this too be discovered. When the shrouds of darkness or doubt shall we say are lifted from one in this form to see his or herself into, then and only then will you shine magnificently bright outwardly from within to the outer exteriors that you are to have held yourself within. Fear not of this undoing from within for it was ever planned to be yours to eventuate into a being of love once more to instil within you a sense of being the lovingness that you are always meant to be. So, stand in your space of illumination that is yours to see yourself in and shine so bright that one will always be hard to miss.

Unique is your divinity that we see you of and in this divinity, we are the complete part of you to be seen into once more.

Always of ours to become.

IN one's aspect or view of themselves to see is to be always in one that is to feel right within. It is to be willing and able to feel a convincing voice to rise from within to know of this worthiness that you are and always shall be. In hesitation it is that we preview the many of you to feel lacking into thoughts of a wellness, strongness, stability and hope to be portrayed by you in a sense of a fear to rise from within in the thinking of this to be yours to feel securely of. It is in this that one must be diligent in his or her words to continue to offer to this being that you are to feel as though you are to be constantly reminded of the power that you possess within this that you are.

You see to others to be of a more-ness or in a better alignment within themselves to be than you.

Do you not?

Why? For it is in only your words, thoughts and physical eyes to see this that you think to be more in another than in oneself to see.

YES, we hear your voice to waver here in a certain weakness or indecision to be offered here in regard to the self to feel enabled to be strong enough or confident enough to be forthcoming with these words in an ability to be more to yourself. Let all hesitations or reservations from the thinkers mind to be offering to you this world of not enough and prepare to make way to clear space within to feel as these words although maybe slow to start or hard to utter will become a wanting to be found so deep and satisfying to you in this creature that you be. You are the one voice of love that unites not only you within yourself to become but to be a strong voice to carry with it a meaningful sound or vibration of love to be heard by yours to beat in time and add a sense of peace and calm and unite many in this time of yours to feel this need to speak, to expand, to grow into this that we describe as the everlasting reminder that one is to be always in remembrance of this that be LOVE…

WE HEAR OF YOU TO ASK; I want to change my view or thoughts but feel unable to do.

We sense of a hesitation here from within to be thinking of this question as to be often asked out of a confused state to be offered that it feels too big of a change that is being asked to start or situation to begin into.

To be felt as all wound up inside and to fear almost everything that you think of yourself to be and in an unwillingness yet also a hardened want from within to feel different or to be offered calm. For it is in this sense of confusion to be emitted from within one is to feel dizzy or uneasiness in a sense in one's lack of peace that one is to feel able to sit into.

One is often as we see; not in a wanting of, so they repeat to say; to sit and to just be, we cannot.

It is often in the thoughts that they are to feel into to see of themselves to be <u>not able to</u> that they are to be contained into this frame of mind and constricted structure to think in this way.

Let yourself be felt first to recognise all that you are to question oneself to be thought of. Feel free to express yourself in words of dismay or thoughts of unjust for often we are to see that these words or thoughts are usually not of your own but constant reminders that you are willing to instil and accept into self to be as seen or offered by circumstance, situations or comments and conversations that one has or is currently having or living into.

You are like sponges we say when it comes to absorbing others energies, dismays and conflicts for it provides the many that seem to be involved in this way or opinions of to be others a lack of willingness to be willing to see into their own concerns to think of. You are never meant to be the consoler of others for many will if allowing of them to come, in droves to speak to you to dump upon you, to provide you with thoughts, dramas, sadness, victims in their own unwillingness to change to be discussed if allowing of them to be.

One is to be in a request to always know that they are to be the guider of self, their shining light to see, knower of them self to be unique to be and in this one must not feel as though it is of theirs to take on board all others offerings to be yours. You will feel a dismay at these words to be offered and we hear you say.

Should I not be CONSIDERATE and KIND of HEART to listen?

In this we offer if it is to create or cause you to much inner stress and emotional upheaval, or dis-ease then <u>NO</u>.

Be okay we say, to say YES to you.

It is not to be neglectful to the loving of others. In this we speak that if you are not to feel right or correct and in balance from within this creature that you are than you will not see to be in a correct place within yourself to offer guidance to those that seem to find unrest within them as they are to speak. One must be in a place of commitment to the self to be accepting of all that are placed in front of you to hear as upon their own deciding of this position or thoughts of to be correct for them. They are drawn to you often witnessed by us in this reasoning that you are to display. One must be in agreeance within self to let them speak if it does not grate upon your soul we would suggest or personally as to upset.

One must be very mindful of their decisions as to who and of what it is that they are to feel in need of to be hearing and interacting with.

In this we do not mean to be selfish to another or to feel selfish in yourself to feel. One is always to be of kind to another although it must be felt out of a genuineness to see only the good that one holds within.

Ask yourself how does this one that speaks or in this that I see make me feel?

THIS SOUNDS HARSH TO HEAR SPOKEN, we hear you speak.

It certainly is to be harsh to hear, for if it is the very first time to be yours to hear into in this your now to listen, it will. Ones such as you in human form love to be involved into certain challenges, dramas, gossip, and lives of others to be willing to offer this from them to be spoken.

IN all aspects of yourself to preview it is in an understanding of it is morally correct of You to be allowing of these conversations to evolve, one should care and take the time to talk, to listen, to solve or offer advice. Should we not?

YOU are the ever producers of your life to be living into and in a want for it to be pleasant, comfortable, safe, unbiased in views of another's one must find first the strength that is theirs from within to be in a place of strongness to speak these words such as.

We offer this; you are all uniquely individual in your thoughts, feelings, opinions or sensing of this self to become. Be bold in this way in which it is to feel, to think, to see and most importantly to speak courageously of oneself as.

* I am not willing to derail myself now from my good thinking thoughts.

* I respect this decision within me to be solo, alone or quiet.

* I need to be by myself for a while.

* I am a deliberate listener to my own thoughts of just and right within me.

* I feel worthy of this time to be mine.

* I am aware that my time is valuable.

* I love your offerings to me, but I have my own opinions that I value more.

* I see you as important to me, but I am choosing to be my important first.

These comments are strong in voice to be spoken I do not feel comfortable to speak them as my own.

There are many we see in a willingness to refuse to speak these comments as theirs to speak, in this we offer find your own that offer you boundaries to be yours to accept in a willingness to find a self-progression to begin. It is not of us to ask you to speak in any certain way, if not to be felt correct within. You are the listener to one's own true heart to speak, so feel words to suit you in this that you be asking of them to be heard.

To feel a sense of worthiness, to be finding the more within you that is crying out to be heard as your completeness to be able to sit into this boldness that you be, shining your own magnificence in an allowance of it to be felt unfolding and blossoming from within. You are the radiant star who beams in all her certainty to become, if only she is allowing of herself or himself to be heard as this your voice of true, compassion, faith and love in your own words to speak, for there is no other that speaks your bold, your kind, your richness.

> Can we ask of you to try in just this moment of your time?

To feel a willingness to compel you to ask of this to speak from within. Be hearing of all that are to speak as one voice to be yours to hear as yours.

It will feel like you are to juggle confusion and a sensing to give up or retreat into what was once known as to feel easier to stay within the conforms of. But in this we say try, try and try again for you will succeed to be ever the MORE that you are to BE.

"THE MORE I SEE MYSELF BEING,
THE MORE I BECOME."

WE ARE WILLING TO SEE YOU
AS THIS THAT YOU ARE

In this to be one's vision to see themselves as this that they are not, then it shall be. Let us speak with certainty to you that this is not how it is that we are to see you. For there is no indecision or doubt to be seen within this ever correct knowing of this that we are to be always a part of. We sense within the many of you to speak your words and in the questions to ask to be shown a willingness from within to be yours to feel, to see, to be this that you are in a want to become of. Let us offer here to you to know that you always are all that you see, feel and BE.

It is not of our choosing to see you in any other way but in your allowing of oneself to feel pulled and constrained from the impressions that you hold onto you will be unable to be in the position it would seem to hear the voice of love that is to speak in all the correct words or knowing for you to hear into. This voice is gallantly yours, courageous and proud in her sensing of this to be you and in this we hear him/her speak much love for you that is resonated and reflected back from us to you as we are to be witness as in the eternalness to be always an image of you to reside into. Let your voice be bold in guidance even if to feel unsure or wavering for your heart feels this space of great intent within you to know as your truth to be. He/she is the one that holds tightly to the truth that you are and in this we offer she will never stray, you are continual movement and expansion to be ever in the loving beings of this that we are.

CHAPTER TEN

~ WE SEE OF YOU HERE ~

It is in us that we see you speak the words that you are to hear. We are forthcoming in offering to be the givers of these words to be felt as yours to speak. One must be thought of as a receiver in all that is to be felt correct within to be able to commute to us in this way. We see the many of you to be in a disregard of self to be thinking as to hear of this that we speak. We are ever known to your heart, your voice of god, your light, your love(however your words are used to express this that we be)within for they are never to be seen as to not know of you to be. They sit in just and quite reasoning of this that you are ever the soldier or guardian of this one to be. So, in this we offer be the most willing to be always in a place of recognition and self-worth to be, be in allowance of the all that is to feel right within you. You are always in the correct place, always to speak the correct words to say, always willing to become this that you are and in this we say that if one is to let go of all resistance that is held within in a tightness to be not allowing of one to be their truth than they will see their own sun shine, be their own truth and never will they disregard their inner knowing, intuition or wisdom not to be felt as real and uniquely their own again. One must be of always an expecting to be more for in this is growth, determination, continual movement forward and a sensing of love is to be the supplier of the ever-ness in eternalness that you are to be.

Worthy of this one must speak these words of themselves to be, you are always seen in the eyes of love and cherishment to be receiving from us this greatness that you are to become. We wish for our message to be to you to always stand in your own unique light and never feel to need another to stand with you. For the lights that are to shine so brightly from within you all are to connect in such a extraordinary way to be seen by us that in this light that beams across the space and into this time that you think of us to be you will one day once again be recognising of this that you be; to be the light that shines so confidently and in correctness as you to be seen and in never any doubt will you think of yourself to be of not enough again upon your willingness to return to us once MORE.

An opportunity to express:

Write upon these pages in freewill of all that you desire yourself to be MORE of. These words written upon these pages will be yours to treasure in certain time of yours to become. Enable oneself to be trusting of all that you are to express, for you are the true speaker, the true teacher, the true seer, the true ancestors of pure wisdom and eternal knowledge within to be heard. She/he is to love of all that you are to recognise from within as a willingness to be written. Reach deeply into your being of this that you are a creation of loving eternalness to be so that you feel this to be spoken as your truth within your heart of hearts to always want for

MORE.

....

....

....

....

....

....

....

....

....
....
....
....
....
....
....
....
....
....
....
....

"We see never no wrong in to always ask for more. It is of this universe and those that are to succeed this one to be. That to be more is always this source in complete knowing to be seen in you."

We sense of you always wanting MORE!

IN this our love so grand to offer you are the grandest version of this self to be seen as, you are the holder of much self-recognition and worth to be forthcoming, allow this to be your truth to be heard as the most loving component of you to be to receive. Live into this life as one in an expectation of self to be always allowing and ever wanting MORE, for you are entitled it would appear to be said that this is yours to receive.

MY message to receive,

There is to be always more to be offered in this way that we are to speak. So, let this be an asking within self to always hear into this voice that is to speak as a difference of yours to be not physical for you are to be the receiver of many more words in truth to express in our voices for you to hear, to write, so that they can be received by the many that are to be in their exact place of wanting to receive.

Final blessings for you to hear;
'I AM' always in a space of recognition of the All that I am to exist into, this worthiness to be envisioning myself as always the bigger component of myself to be the part that always in her willingness is to stand into the light of this love that is decidedly mine to express myself as. And in your truth to be heard I know that you will be too. Let our lights be always a brightness that is to shine as one. Always to recognise each other in every aspect to be. To be always felt as more to each other in this that we stand together to share this message spoken in LOVE.

My spirits essence that stands so proudly seen is to respond to this in all that I see as me in you, feel never not willing to be capable to dream yourself of bigness and a grand to see. You are here to illuminate this earth and her people to progress forth out of a sense of insecurity to be felt to express themselves as a love so magnificent to see. Let down all your walls of constraint so that one may be always tempted to shine outwardly from the innerness held within in a divine expression of this soul to be felt as you, in this place of absolute presence to be spoken of as your NOW to see you BOLD, LOVED and full of FAITH again to recognise as this the sovereign being of love & radiant light that you

Always Blessed

www.ingramcontent.com/pod-product-compliance
Lightning Source LLC
Chambersburg PA
CBHW070307010526
44107CB00056B/2513